T0335006

THE 23RD PSALM

THE LORD, OUR SHEPHERD

JUANITA RYAN

9 STUDIES FOR INDIVIDUALS OR GROUPS

ivp

Life Builder Study

INTER-VARSITY PRESS
36 Causton Street, London SW1P 4ST, England
Email: ivp@ivpbooks.com
Website: www.ivpbooks.com

*Originally published in the United States of America in the LifeGuide® Bible Studies series
in 2006 by InterVarsity Press, Downers Grove, Illinois*
Second edition published 2015
First published in Great Britain by Scripture Union in 2006
This edition published in Great Britain by Inter-Varsity Press 2018

British Library Cataloguing-in-Publication Data
A catalogue record for this book is available from the British Library.

ISBN: 978–1–78359–814–4

Printed in Great Britain by Ashford Colour Ltd, Gosport, Hampshire

*Inter-Varsity Press publishes Christian books that are true to the Bible and that communicate
the gospel, develop discipleship and strengthen the church for its mission in the world.*

*IVP originated within the Inter-Varsity Fellowship, now the Universities and Colleges Christian
Fellowship, a student movement connecting Christian Unions in universities and colleges
throughout Great Britain, and a member movement of the International Fellowship of
Evangelical Students. Website: www.uccf.org.uk. That historic association is maintained,
and all senior IVP staff and committee members subscribe to the UCCF Basis of Faith.*

Contents

Getting the Most Out of
The 23rd Psalm

Psalm 23 pictures life as deeply secure and richly blessed. It offers us a panorama of what life can be like when lived with awareness of God's intimate love for us. This picture of life lived in God's care touches our deepest longings and speaks directly to our darkest fears. Perhaps that is why we return to this psalm over and over again.

It is possible, however, that our frequent exposure may actually result in our becoming too familiar with this jewel. We may read it and not fully hear its sweet, strong message. We may miss the key it offers to a life well lived. The purpose of this study guide is to help you to look again at this psalm. The studies will help you to take time with the beauty and wisdom that are here. Most importantly, these studies will help you to see God through the psalmist's eyes. You will have an opportunity to reflect deeply on the God who is our good Shepherd so that your heart and mind will be nourished and your soul will be restored.

Psalm 23 is a personal confession of love and gratitude from one human soul to God. It is a portrait of a God who is astonishingly intimate, kind, protective and generous with us. The message it offers, the golden key it holds out to us is this: we are invited to live securely in God's love and care for us. We are sheep—not very strong, not very wise, very much in need of help and guidance. God is a good Shepherd. God tends to us, cares for us, plans for us, provides for us, protects us, guides us and stays close to us. In life and in death we can come to know that all is well because God, our good Shepherd, is with us. Our part is to remember who we are and who God is. Our part is to rest in God's unfailing love, to follow God's faithful guidance and to allow ourselves to receive our good Shepherd's personal care for us.

The meaning, purpose and satisfaction we search for in life does not come from striving or proving ourselves or working hard to please others or God. The simple secret explored in this psalm is that life becomes rich, full and deeply satisfying when we rest in God's unfailing love.

May your heart and mind be nourished in the green pastures and beside the quiet waters of God's kindness. May your soul be restored as you grow in awareness of God's personal, tender care for you. May you rest in the promise of God's constant presence with you. May you know the peace and joy that come in anticipating that God's love and goodness will follow you all the days of your life. May you find your true home in the God who delights in you and who loves you unconditionally, abundantly and faithfully.

Suggestions for Individual Study

1. As you begin each study, pray that God will speak to you through his Word.

2. Read the introduction to the study and respond to the personal reflection question or exercise. This is designed to help you focus on God and on the theme of the study.

3. Each study deals with a particular passage—so that you can delve into the author's meaning in that context. Read and reread the passage to be studied. The questions are written using the language of the New International Version, so you may wish to use that version of the Bible. The New Revised

Standard Version is also recommended.

4. This is an inductive Bible study, designed to help you discover for yourself what Scripture is saying. The study includes three types of questions. *Observation* questions ask about the basic facts: who, what, when, where and how. *Interpretation* questions delve into the meaning of the passage. *Application* questions help you discover the implications of the text for growing in Christ. These three keys unlock the treasures of Scripture.

Write your answers to the questions in the spaces provided or in a personal journal. Writing can bring clarity and deeper understanding of yourself and of God's Word.

5. It might be good to have a Bible dictionary handy. Use it to look up any unfamiliar words, names or places.

6. Use the prayer suggestion to guide you in thanking God for what you have learned and to pray about the applications that have come to mind.

7. You may want to go on to the suggestion under "Now or Later," or you may want to use that idea for your next study.

Suggestions for Members of a Group Study

1. Come to the study prepared. Follow the suggestions for individual study mentioned above. You will find that careful preparation will greatly enrich your time spent in group discussion.

2. Be willing to participate in the discussion. The leader of your group will not be lecturing. Instead, he or she will be encouraging the members of the group to discuss what they have learned. The leader will be asking the questions that are found in this guide.

3. Stick to the topic being discussed. Your answers should be based on the verses which are the focus of the discussion and not on outside authorities such as commentaries or speakers.

These studies focus on a particular passage of Scripture. Only rarely should you refer to other portions of the Bible. This allows for everyone to participate in in-depth study on equal ground.

4. Be sensitive to the other members of the group. Listen attentively when they describe what they have learned. You may be surprised by their insights! Each question assumes a variety of answers. Many questions do not have "right" answers, particularly questions that aim at meaning or application. Instead the questions push us to explore the passage more thoroughly.

When possible, link what you say to the comments of others. Also, be affirming whenever you can. This will encourage some of the more hesitant members of the group to participate.

5. Be careful not to dominate the discussion. We are sometimes so eager to express our thoughts that we leave too little opportunity for others to respond. By all means participate! But allow others to also.

6. Expect God to teach you through the passage being discussed and through the other members of the group. Pray that you will have an enjoyable and profitable time together, but also that as a result of the study you will find ways that you can take action individually and/or as a group.

7. Remember that anything said in the group is considered confidential and should not be discussed outside the group unless specific permission is given to do so.

8. If you are the group leader, you will find additional suggestions at the back of the guide.

1

The God Who Shepherds Us

Psalm 23 is written from the perspective of a shepherd in Palestine. It was his job to take the family's flock of sheep out in search of food. This meant going on long journeys with the sheep. It meant living with the sheep day and night. It meant guarding them from predators. It meant finding suitable pastures for them to graze and enough water for them to drink.

Being a shepherd meant thinking about the needs of the flock most of the time—much like a parent thinks about the needs of a young child, planning ahead for feeding time and rest time and play time. I remember when I was caring for our children when they were little, anticipating their needs and delighting in their presence in our home, I would find myself reflecting from time to time, "this is a picture of what God does for me." As the psalmist cared for his flock, he seems to have had a similar experience.

GROUP DISCUSSION. When have you experienced joy in meeting a need for someone?

PERSONAL REFLECTION. What would you list as your most basic five or six needs in life?

The psalmist sees in his experience of delighting in and providing for his beloved sheep a picture of the loving, active, intimate care that God provides day after day all through our lives. He wrote as one whose eyes are opened to the amazing truth of God's powerful, protective, joyful, sustaining love for us. *Read Psalm 23.*

---

1. The thesis for this psalm is stated in the first verse. How would you paraphrase this verse for our context?

---

2. List the needs that God the Shepherd meets as they are described in the rest of this psalm.

---

3. We live in a consumer society. We tend to think of ourselves as always lacking something, always needing something more. Reflect for a moment on what it would be like to be aware that God will provide everything you need. What thoughts and feelings do you have as you reflect on this thought?

4. Which of the needs identified in this psalm are you particularly aware of God meeting in your life at this time?

5. What is it like for you to experience God's care in this way?

6. Which of the provisions described in this psalm are you especially in need of?

7. This psalm describes our relationship with God as one in which God actively provides for us. God gives and cares and attends. We receive and receive and receive. How does this picture of God compare with your concept and experience of God?

8. Sheep are vulnerable animals, in need of their shepherd's care. In what ways do you relate to this metaphor of being a sheep?

9. How does this picture of who we are in relationship to God (the receivers of love and care) compare with your concept of who you are in relationship to God?

10. What difference might it make (or does it make) in your life to see your relationship with God in this way?

11. Do you relate to the image of God as a shepherd? What other images come to mind when you reflect on God as the one who provides, cares, protects and guides?

12. Spend a few minutes in quiet, reflecting on God as your loving shepherd or caretaker. What thoughts and feelings or images come to you as you reflect in this way?

---

13. When we are experiencing a specific need, it can be helpful to remember that God, who is our loving Shepherd, desires to meet our needs. Scripture frequently reminds us to talk to God about our needs. What specific needs are you experiencing at this time that you would like to ask God to meet?

Express your needs and your gratitude to God who shepherds you.

Now or Later

This week, begin each day in quiet, reflecting on God as your loving Shepherd. End each day by focusing on the ways you sense that God cared for you during the day.

You might want to keep a gratitude list, acknowledging God's specific care each day.

Pray that your heart and mind will be open to receive all the good gifts God is giving you.

2

The God Who
Invites Us to Rest

The first item on the list of provisions given to us by God our Shepherd is rest. It is easy to read right past this truth every time we encounter this psalm. The reality is that sheep, much like many humans, do not easily rest. If left to themselves they tend to wander aimlessly. They will not lie down unless they have a readily available supply of food. And, because they are defenseless and vulnerable, once they do lie down, they tend to be quite skittish. A small sound or movement can send them running.*

But a good shepherd knows all this about his sheep. And so, he finds rich pastures and leads them there. And he directs them to stop and rest. He also stays with them to calm and reassure them.

GROUP DISCUSSION. What images come to mind when you think about resting?

PERSONAL REFLECTION. Describe a time when you experienced emotional and spiritual rest.

Read Psalm 23:2-3.

"He makes me lie down in green pastures,
he leads me beside quiet waters,
   he restores my soul."

---

1. These verses tell us about a God who causes us to lie down in green pastures, who leads us beside quiet waters and who restores our soul. Take a minute of quiet to reflect on these images. What thoughts and feelings do you have in response to these images?

---

2. *Read Matthew 11:25-30.* This text begins with Jesus praying. In his prayer, Jesus emphasizes the importance of spiritual humility (being little children). What is the relationship between spiritual humility and being able to respond to an invitation to rest?

---

3. What does Jesus invite us to do in the text from Matthew?

4. What promises does Jesus make?

5. How do these promises compare with your expectations of what Jesus wants to offer you or expects from you?

6. What words would you use to paraphrase the way Jesus describes himself in the text from Matthew?

7. What about this description of Jesus might make it easier to rest in Jesus' presence?

8. Psalm 23:3 says that the rest God provides "restores my soul." In Matthew 11:29 Jesus promises "rest for your souls." What do you think these phrases mean?

9. What experiences have you had of your soul needing rest?

---

10. The text in Matthew is addressed to people who are weary and burdened. What is causing you to feel weary and burdened at this time in your life?

---

11. What makes it difficult for you to rest physically, emotionally, spiritually?

---

12. What helps you to rest physically, emotionally and spiritually?

---

13. Take a few minutes of quiet and picture yourself in a green meadow, beside quiet waters with Jesus. Jesus has invited you to come to him and to rest with him. You have accepted the invitation. As you rest quietly with Jesus, he reminds you that you are safe with him because he is gentle and humble in heart.

Write about your experience during this time of reflection.

Respond honestly to Jesus' invitation to rest. Share your fears, your hesitations, your longings, your gratitude, your need for help in resting, your need for rest or whatever honest responses you have.

Now or Later

This week reread Matthew 11:28-30. Revisit question 13, writing each day about your experience as you respond to Jesus' invitation to rest.

---

*Haddon W. Robinson, *Trusting the Shepherd* (Grand Rapids: Discovery House Publishers, 1968), p. 35.

3

The God Who Guides Us

Psalm 25

In a flock of sheep there are always some who wander away. Some sheep become distracted and lose their way. Some sheep want to go their own way. But the shepherd knows this and looks out for them, drawing them back onto the path.

God does not expect us to travel alone through life. God stays with us. A good shepherd anticipates and plans for the needs of his sheep. God goes before us and beside us, guiding us on the right path.

GROUP DISCUSSION. What images come to mind when you think of a shepherd guiding his sheep?

PERSONAL REFLECTION. Think of a time you experienced a sense of guidance from God. Describe the experience.

Seeking and following God's loving, personal guidance for our lives is central to the life of serenity and peace that is portrayed in Psalm 23. It is also the deep heart cry of David in Psalm 25:4, "Show me your ways, O LORD."

Read Psalm 23:3.
"He guides me in paths of righteousness
  for his name's sake."

Read Psalm 25.

---

1. What emotions do you see being expressed directly and indirectly in Psalm 25?

---

2. When have you been in a situation in which you needed God's guidance in the way that is expressed here?

---

3. How does the psalmist describe his relationship with God (vv. 1, 5, 7, 9, 11, 15-16, 20-21)?

4. As you look at your answer to question 3, how would you compare or contrast the psalmist's relationship with God and your relationship with God at this time?

---

5. What does the psalmist say about God?

---

6. What does the psalmist ask of God?

---

7. How might the reassurance of God's provision of guidance found in Psalm 23 provide comfort to a person seeking God's guidance with the urgency found in Psalm 25?

---

8. As you look at your answer to question 5, how would you compare or contrast what the psalmist trusted to be true about God and what you trust to be true about God?

9. In Psalm 25 the writer comes back to his need for forgiveness and God's forgiving love several times (vv. 6-9, 11, 18). What thoughts do you have about the relationship between this theme and the theme of seeking God's guidance?

---

10. Many of us can identify with the sheep who stray. What fears or beliefs make it difficult for you to seek and follow God's guidance at times?

---

11. What needs do you have for guidance at this time?

Pray, inviting God to guide you.

Now or Later

Begin each day this week asking God for guidance and thanking God for the promise of guidance. End each day reflecting on the ways you can see God guiding you. If this is a struggle for you, spend time each day praying that God will heal your fears and open your eyes and heart to God's love so that your desire for God's guidance can grow.

4

The God Who Is with Us

Sheep are defenseless creatures. They have no ability to protect themselves. They cannot even be trusted to find food on their own or to rest when they are tired, much less to defend themselves from attacks of predators. Sheep need the constant protection of their shepherd.

When sheep in Palestine are on their journey to the high meadows they pass through deep canyons, which are dark and filled with dangers.* While in these dark valleys the shepherd is especially close, always making his presence known.

GROUP DISCUSSION. When children are frightened in the middle of the night, what they need more than anything is someone to be with them. They need someone to reassure them with their presence. Think of a time you were afraid as a child. Describe your experience.

PERSONAL REFLECTION. Think of a time when you were afraid and experienced God being with you. Describe your experience.

In Psalm 34 David describes his experience of facing dangers and threats of every kind, of being afflicted and even broken-hearted. In spite of the experiences of affliction acknowledged in this psalm, this psalm is a psalm of good news, of loud shouts of praise, for David tells of discovering that God was with him—that God responded to his calls for help and rescued him.

Read Psalm 23:4.
"Even though I walk
   through the valley of the shadow of death,
I will fear no evil,
   For you are with me."

Read Psalm 34.

---

1. What title would you give Psalm 34?

---

2. List all the things the psalmist says that God has done and continues to do for us in Psalm 34.

---

3. What response does the psalmist have in these verses to all the ways in which God has been with him?

4. The first verse of Psalm 34 tells us that this psalm is meant especially for those who are *afflicted*. The psalm is written to encourage us when we are in distress or when we are walking through a dark valley. Reflect for a moment on the afflictions or dark valleys you have experienced in life. What have those times been like for you?

———————————————————————————

5. What invitations and instructions do you find in this psalm?

———————————————————————————

6. Both Psalm 34:19 and Psalm 23:4 teach us to expect difficult times, even when we are following God's ways. How does this compare with your expectations?

———————————————————————————

7. Verses 17-19 tell us that the righteous may have many troubles, but that God will be close to them in those troubles and will deliver them. Have you found this to be true? What is your response to these verses?

8. How might God make his presence known to us? What helps you experience God's presence?

---

9. Take a minute of quiet and ask God to show you how he is with you as your refuge and help. Write whatever thoughts and feelings come to you.

Talk to God about whatever troubles you are experiencing. Invite God to show you that God's Spirit is with you always.

Now or Later

Begin each day this week by reflecting on the truth that God will be with you all day, even in the difficulties. Invite God each day to remind you of his Spirit's presence with you. End each day by reflecting on the times you were aware of God's presence.

---

*Phillip Keller, *A Shepherd Looks at Psalm 23* (Grand Rapids: Zondervan, 1970), p. 75.

5

The God Who Comforts Us

Isaiah 40:9-11, 25-31

"Your rod and your staff comfort me." This well-known phrase may seem strange at first reading. But in the context we have just explored—that God is with us through dangers of every kind—this phrase takes on deep meaning. The psalmist is saying that God comforts him with his power and with his loving presence.

The shepherd's rod is a weapon of defense. It is designed to defend against predators. The shepherd's ability to use the rod to protect the sheep from predators is the sheep's only hope for survival from attack. The rod, then, can be seen as a symbol of God's power in caring for us.*

The shepherd's staff is used to pull sheep out of gullies and ditches and to guide them along the path. The shepherd also uses his staff to gently connect with his sheep, allowing the staff to rest on the sheep's side as it walks along, as if to say "I am here with you." The staff, then, can be seen as a symbol of God's kindness in caring for us.†

Nothing is more comforting to us in times of need than the presence of someone who loves us—especially when that someone is powerful enough to protect us and help us.

GROUP DISCUSSION. Think of a time when you felt comforted by another person. What did they do that caused you to feel comforted?

PERSONAL REFLECTION. Think of a time you felt comforted by God. Describe your experience.

Read Psalm 23:4.
"Your rod and your staff,
    they comfort me."
Read Isaiah 40:9-11, 25-31.

1. This section of Isaiah 40 begins by saying that it is a declaration of good tidings. What are the good tidings in this text?

2. How do these passages in Isaiah 40 describe God?

3. What thoughts and feelings do you have as you read these descriptions of God?

4. In what ways is God's power important to you when you need comfort?

5. Isaiah 40:11 describes God as a tender shepherd. In what ways is God's tender, loving presence important to you when you need comfort?

6. How do the images of God's power and tenderness in this text compare or contrast with your own expectations of God?

7. What specific comfort do you need from God at this time?

8. How might God's rod bring comfort to you?

9. How might God's staff bring comfort to you?

10. How do the images in Isaiah 40:29-31 describe what can take place in our lives when we receive comfort from God?

11. Which of these images best describes your current experience?

Spend some time thanking God for being a God of comfort.

Now or Later

Take a few minutes of quiet to put yourself into this passage and experience God's power and God's tender love for you. Allow yourself to receive comfort from God. Write about your experience during this time of reflection.

Bring all your needs for comfort to God each day this week. Use the images from these passages to help you take in God's comfort and care.

---

*Phillip Keller, *A Shepherd Looks at Psalm 23* (Grand Rapids: Zondervan, 1970), p. 93.
†Ibid., pp. 94-97.

6

The God Who Feeds Us

Isaiah 55

Psalm 23 states that God prepares a table for us in the presence of our enemies. We may read this as a literal table on which dinner is served. Or we may see this as the pastures found on the high tablelands where shepherds take their sheep for the best summer grazing.* Either way, it is a picture of God who feeds us.

God offers to feed us and quench our thirst with his deep love for us. God wants no less for us than the very best spiritual food and drink.

But we may have lost awareness of our spiritual hunger and thirst. We may have despaired long ago that real love will ever be ours. We may cover our despair and the hunger that is beneath it with trying hard to be good and look good. Or we may act out of our despair in ways that are self-destructive, filling our lives with things that do not satisfy.

God calls us with great love to come and feed at the banquet table prepared for us. God calls us to feel our thirst and our hunger for God and to come empty-handed—penniless—to God's free, extravagant feast.

GROUP DISCUSSION. Imagine a person coming to the end of their life. What kind of life experiences would a person near the end of life most likely describe as deeply satisfying?

PERSONAL REFLECTION. Reflect back over the past week or two. What experiences have left you feeling empty? What experiences have been deeply satisfying emotionally and spiritually?

Read Psalm 23:5.
"You prepare a table before me
in the presence of my enemies."

Read Isaiah 55.

---

1. Psalm 23:5 tells us that God prepares food for us. What responses do you have to the thought of God wanting to provide you with nurture?

---

2. Psalm 23:5 states that God feeds us in the presence of our enemies. What enemies (perhaps spiritual) are you aware of in your life?

---

3. Isaiah 55:2 asks us why we would spend money on what does not satisfy. How do your enemies tempt you with things that do not satisfy?

4. What would it be like to think of yourself eating peacefully and richly at God's banquet table, aware that God is protecting you?

5. What does Isaiah 55 tell us about God?

6. What are we invited and instructed to do in this text?

7. Describe a time when you were aware of God providing emotional or spiritual nurture to you.

8. What is the "good" that God wants to feed us (Isaiah 55:2)?

9. Isaiah 55:7 describes God's mercy and pardon. How is the experience of receiving God's mercy part of the experience of being fed by God?

10. Isaiah 55:12 describes gifts of joy and peace. In your experience what is the connection between experiencing joy and peace and being nurtured by God?

11. Isaiah 55:2 God invites each of us to come to God and to experience our "soul delighting in the richest of fare." Take a minute of quiet to put yourself in this picture and to reflect on this image. What thoughts and feelings do you have as you reflect?

Ask God to increase your spiritual hunger. Ask God to increase your appetite for spiritual nurture.

Now or Later

Take time each day this week to reflect and pray in two ways. First, ask God to show you what are you consuming that is not satisfying to your soul. Second, picture yourself sitting at a banquet table prepared for you by God. Imagine yourself being loved and nurtured by God. What spiritual food do you sense that God is offering you?

Keep a journal about your thoughts and experiences each day as you pray and reflect in these ways.

---

*Phillip Keller, A Shepherd Looks at Psalm 23 (Grand Rapids: Zondervan, 1970), p. 99.

7

The God Who Heals Us

Isaiah 61:1-3

"You anoint my head with oil." This familiar biblical image is rich with possible meanings. Kings, prophets and priests were anointed with oil as a sign that they were chosen by God. Guests were greeted and welcomed with foot washing and with their heads being anointed with oil. People who were sick were anointed with oil to bring them healing.*

In the world of the shepherd, anointing with oil was medicinal. Oil was the healing ointment used by the shepherd to protect the sheep from insects that could be ferocious in their attack on the sheep and also to treat wounds the sheep might experience.†

The text for this study tells us of one who is anointed by God and who, like a good shepherd, will heal our deepest wounds—replacing our ashes of grief and despair with the oil of gladness.

GROUP DISCUSSION. Think of a time when you or someone you know recovered from an illness. What feelings did the recovery produce in the person who recovered?

PERSONAL REFLECTION. What healing have you experienced from God (physically, emotionally or spiritually)?

Read Psalm 23:5.
"You anoint my head with oil;
my cup overflows."

Read Isaiah 61:1-3.

1. What title would you give the text in Isaiah 61:1-3?

2. List all the things this text suggests God's anointed One will do.

3. Jesus read this text in the temple as he began his ministry. He said this prophecy was being fulfilled as he read. Jesus was the anointed One spoken of in this passage. How do you see this as a description of Jesus' life and work?

4. Think of times when you have had experiences of being poor (financially, spiritually or any other way), or broken-hearted, or in prison (physically, emotionally or spiritually). What were those times like for you?

5. What thoughts and feelings (positive or negative) do you have as you read the promises of help and healing in this passage?

6. How does this image of God as the God who heals us compare to your sense of who God is?

7. Look at the contrasts in Isaiah 61:3. Use your own words to describe the "before" and "after" images found in this verse.

8. Psalm 23:5 uses an image of joy following the image of anointing. "My cup overflows." How does this image compare with the "after" images in Isaiah 61:3?

9. Both of these passages remind us that God's healing leads to joy. How have you seen this to be true in your own life?

10. What healing do you need to receive from God at this time?

11. Which of the images and promises from these two passages (Psalm 23:5 and Isaiah 61:1-3) speak to you most powerfully today?

Spend some time thanking God for being a God who heals. Invite God to heal you physically, emotionally, spiritually and relationally.

Now or Later

Take a few moments of quiet to reflect on the images and promises in this text that speak the most to you at this time. Use as many of your senses as you can (visual, auditory, tactile) to experience the images of help and healing. Write about your experience during this time of reflection.

Reread these texts each day and use question 11 for a time of reflection, focusing on different images each day if you choose. Write about your time of reflection each day.

*Geoffrey W. Bromiley, ed., *The International Standard Bible Encyclopedia* (Grand Rapids: Eerdmans, 1979), p. 586.
†Phillip Keller, *A Shepherd Looks at Psalm 23* (Grand Rapids: Zondervan, 1970), pp. 113, 117.

8

The God Who Blesses Us

Psalm 40

"Surely goodness and love will follow me / all the days of my life."

What an extraordinary picture of the future. The psalmist looks into his future and rests in the awareness that his life will continue to be blessed with God's goodness and love. The psalmist understood that just as God had cared for him in the past, and cares for him in the present, God would continue to care for him, blessing his life with goodness and love all the days of his life.

Many of us have a very different experience when we look into the future. We may find ourselves looking into the future and experiencing fear instead of the hope the psalmist possessed. We may anticipate that things will be terrible in some way. What a difference it would make in our daily experience to look into the future and anticipate that, in all circumstances of life, we will continue to be blessed by God's goodness and love.

GROUP DISCUSSION. Give an example of what it might mean to bless someone.

PERSONAL REFLECTION. Of all the ways God has blessed you, what one or two blessings touch you the most deeply?

The basis of hope for the future is the same as the hope for the present. Psalm 23 and Psalm 40 teach us that our hope for peace in life is based in the extraordinary promise of God's loving presence with us all the days of our lives.

Read Psalm 23:6.
"Surely goodness and love will follow me
    all the days of my life."

---

1. How would you paraphrase the statement in the first part of Psalm 23:6?

What is your gut-level response to this verse? Do you believe it? Why or why not?

---

2. *Read Psalm 40.* What does the psalmist say God has done for him (vv. 2-3)?

3. What is your response to the psalmist's description in verse 5 of God's bountiful blessings?

4. In verse 4 the psalmist offers important advice. When he was waiting for God to act, he could have taken matters into his own hands. Describe a time when you took matters into your own hands. What happened?

5. Describe a time when you waited, prayed and trusted (Psalm 40:1, 4). What happened?

6. Psalm 40:6-8 describes a significant insight the psalmist has gained. The expression "my ears have you pierced" refers to being able to hear and understand in a new way. How would you paraphrase the insight that is shared in these verses?

7. The tone of the text turns at Psalm 40:11. What is the psalmist expressing in verses 11-17?

How does this section fit with the verses of praise (40:1-10)?

8. The first part of Psalm 23:6 is a statement of hope. It is a statement about the future. Psalm 40:5 also talks about the things God has planned for us. At the same time Psalm 40:12 says, "troubles without number surround me." What can you learn about prayer in times of trouble from the psalmist's model here?

9. In Psalm 40:2-3, 5 the psalmist talks about his gratitude for God's endless blessings in his life. Take a few minutes to make a gratitude list, thanking God for everything that comes to mind.

10. In Psalm 40:9-10 the psalmist talks about expressing his gratitude for God to others. How would you like to express your gratitude for God's blessings to others?

Thank God for being a God who blesses you and who plans to bless you with goodness and love all the days of your life.

Now or Later

Each day this week end the day by writing a gratitude list, thanking God for the blessings of the day.

Take some time each day to think about your future (next week, next year or the next decade) being blessed by God's goodness and love, every day, all the days of your life.

9

The God Who
Is Our True Home

Psalm 16

Home. A place of quiet refuge. A place where we enjoy true connectedness with others. This is what we want our physical homes to offer us. It is also what our spirits long for. But where do we go to find rest and safety and true companionship for our soul? Where is our spirit's true home?

GROUP DISCUSSION. What is a true home like? Perhaps your childhood home comes to mind or a grandparent's home or a friend's home. Describe the place that most feels like home to you.

PERSONAL REFLECTION. What thoughts and feelings come to you when you reflect on God as your true home?

The psalmist responds to our heart's longing by reminding us that God is our refuge, that God is our dwelling place, that God is our true home. God is with us, always. We live in God, who loves us and actively cares for us. It is God who is our soul's true home now and forever. This basic truth is the very essence of Psalm 23. It is the reason this intimate song of loving gratitude was written.

Read Psalm 23:6
"I will dwell in the house of the LORD
    forever."

Read Psalm 16.

1. List who the psalmist says God is to him and what he says God does (and will do) for him.

2. What does Psalm 16 tell us about God?

3. How does the picture of God's character in this psalm compare with your image of God?

4. Notice Psalm 16:3. What is the psalmist saying here? In what way do you relate to this experience?

5. In Psalm 16:5-6 the psalmist says that God has given him security and a "delightful inheritance." How has this been true for you (physically, emotionally or spiritually)?

6. Which of the psalmist's statements give you a sense of his experience of God as his true home here in this life?

7. Which of these statements (from question 6) do you not relate to?

8. Which of these statements (from question 6) do you most relate to?

9. What experiences have allowed you to see God as your true home in this life?

10. Which of the psalmist's statements give you a sense of his view that God is his true home for all eternity?

11. What does the psalmist say or do to respond to God in this psalm?

12. Read Psalm 16:11 and the last statement of Psalm 23. In a moment of quiet, reflect on all that Psalm 23 says about the character of God. As you reflect on the God who is your good Shepherd, reflect on what it might mean to live in close, intimate relationship with God forever. Write about your experience in this time of reflection.

Talk to God who is your true home. Tell God whatever thoughts and feelings you have about your desire to know God in this way, or your gratitude for the sense you have of God as your true home.

Now or Later

Reflect this week on the God who is your true home now and forever. Take time to journal your responses and reflections each day.

Leader's Notes

MY GRACE IS SUFFICIENT FOR YOU. (2 COR 12:9)

Leading a Bible discussion can be an enjoyable and rewarding experience. But it can also be *scary*—especially if you've never done it before. If this is your feeling, you're in good company. When God asked Moses to lead the Israelites out of Egypt, he replied, "O LORD, please send someone else to do it" (Ex 4:13). It was the same with Solomon, Jeremiah and Timothy, but God helped these people in spite of their weaknesses, and he will help you as well.

You don't need to be an expert on the Bible or a trained teacher to lead a Bible discussion. The idea behind these inductive studies is that the leader guides group members to discover for themselves what the Bible has to say. This method of learning will allow group members to remember much more of what is said than a lecture would.

These studies are designed to be led easily. As a matter of fact, the flow of questions through the passage from observation to interpretation to application is so natural that you may feel that the studies lead themselves. This study guide is also flexible. You can use it with a variety of groups—student, professional, neighborhood or church groups. Each study takes forty-five to sixty minutes in a group setting.

There are some important facts to know about group dynamics and encouraging discussion. The suggestions listed below should enable you to effectively and enjoyably fulfill your role as leader.

Preparing for the Study

1. Ask God to help you understand and apply the passage in your

own life. Unless this happens, you will not be prepared to lead others. Pray too for the various members of the group. Ask God to open your hearts to the message of his Word and motivate you to action.

2. Read the introduction to the entire guide to get an overview of the entire book and the issues which will be explored.

3. As you begin each study, read and reread the assigned Bible passage to familiarize yourself with it.

4. This study guide is based on the New International Version of the Bible. It will help you and the group if you use this translation as the basis for your study and discussion.

5. Carefully work through each question in the study. Spend time in meditation and reflection as you consider how to respond.

6. Write your thoughts and responses in the space provided in the study guide. This will help you to express your understanding of the passage clearly.

7. It might help to have a Bible dictionary handy. Use it to look up any unfamiliar words, names or places. (For additional help on how to study a passage, see chapter five of *How to Lead a LifeBuilder Study*, IVP, 2018.)

8. Consider how you can apply the Scripture to your life. Remember that the group will follow your lead in responding to the studies. They will not go any deeper than you do.

9. Once you have finished your own study of the passage, familiarize yourself with the leader's notes for the study you are leading. These are designed to help you in several ways. First, they tell you the purpose the study guide author had in mind when writing the study. Take time to think through how the study questions work together to accomplish that purpose. Second, the notes provide you with additional background information or suggestions on group dynamics for various questions. This information can be useful when people have difficulty understanding or answering a question. Third, the leader's notes can alert you to potential problems you may encounter during the study.

10. If you wish to remind yourself of anything mentioned in the leader's notes, make a note to yourself below that question in the study.

Leading the Study

1. Begin the study on time. Open with prayer, asking God to help the group to understand and apply the passage.

2. Be sure that everyone in your group has a study guide. Encourage the group to prepare beforehand for each discussion by reading the introduction to the guide and by working through the questions in the study.

3. At the beginning of your first time together, explain that these studies are meant to be discussions, not lectures. Encourage the members of the group to participate. However, do not put pressure on those who may be hesitant to speak during the first few sessions. You may want to suggest the following guidelines to your group.

☐ Stick to the topic being discussed.

☐ Your responses should be based on the verses which are the focus of the discussion and not on outside authorities such as commentaries or speakers.

☐ These studies focus on a particular passage of Scripture. Only rarely should you refer to other portions of the Bible. This allows for everyone to participate in in-depth study on equal ground.

☐ Anything said in the group is considered confidential and will not be discussed outside the group unless specific permission is given to do so.

☐ We will listen attentively to each other and provide time for each person present to talk.

☐ We will pray for each other.

4. Have a group member read the introduction at the beginning of the discussion.

5. Every session begins with a group discussion question. The question or activity is meant to be used before the passage is read. The question introduces the theme of the study and encourages group members to begin to open up. Encourage as many members as possible to participate, and be ready to get the discussion going with your own response.

This section is designed to reveal where our thoughts or feelings need to be transformed by Scripture. That is why it is especially important not to read the passage before the discussion question is asked. The passage will tend to color the honest reactions people would otherwise give because they are, of course, supposed to think the way the Bible does.

You may want to supplement the group discussion question with an icebreaker to help people to get comfortable. See the community section of the *Small Group Starter Kit* (IVP, 1995) for more ideas.

You also might want to use the personal reflection question with your group. Either allow a time of silence for people to respond individually or discuss it together.

6. Have a group member (or members if the passage is long) read aloud the passage to be studied. Then give people several minutes to read the passage again silently so that they can take it all in.

7. Question 1 will generally be an overview question designed to briefly survey the passage. Encourage the group to look at the whole passage, but try to avoid getting sidetracked by questions or issues that will be addressed later in the study.

8. As you ask the questions, keep in mind that they are designed to be used just as they are written. You may simply read them aloud. Or you may prefer to express them in your own words.

There may be times when it is appropriate to deviate from the study guide. For example, a question may have already been answered. If so, move on to the next question. Or someone may raise an important question not covered in the guide. Take time to discuss it, but try to keep the group from going off on tangents.

9. Avoid answering your own questions. If necessary, repeat or rephrase them until they are clearly understood. Or point out something you read in the leader's notes to clarify the context or meaning. An eager group quickly becomes passive and silent if they think the leader will do most of the talking.

10. Don't be afraid of silence. People may need time to think about the question before formulating their answers.

11. Don't be content with just one answer. Ask, "What do the rest of you think?" or "Anything else?" until several people have given answers to the question.

12. Acknowledge all contributions. Try to be affirming whenever possible. Never reject an answer. If it is clearly off-base, ask, "Which verse led you to that conclusion?" or again, "What do the rest of you think?"

13. Don't expect every answer to be addressed to you, even though this will probably happen at first. As group members become more at ease, they will begin to truly interact with each other. This is one sign of healthy discussion.

14. Don't be afraid of controversy. It can be very stimulating. If you don't resolve an issue completely, don't be frustrated. Move on and keep it in mind for later. A subsequent study may solve the problem.

15. Periodically summarize what the group has said about the passage. This helps to draw together the various ideas mentioned and gives continuity to the study. But don't preach.

16. At the end of the Bible discussion you may want to allow group members a time of quiet to work on an idea under "Now or Later." Then discuss what you experienced. Or you may want to encourage group members to work on these ideas between meetings. Give an opportunity during the session for people to talk about what they are learning.

17. Conclude your time together with conversational prayer, adapting the prayer suggestion at the end of the study to your group. Ask for God's help in following through on the commitments you've made.

18. End on time.

Many more suggestions and helps are found in *How to Lead a LifeBuilder Study*.

Components of Small Groups

A healthy small group should do more than study the Bible. There are four components to consider as you structure your time together.

Nurture. Small groups help us to grow in our knowledge and love of God. Bible study is the key to making this happen and is the foundation of your small group.

Community. Small groups are a great place to develop deep friendships with other Christians. Allow time for informal interaction before and after each study. Plan activities and games that will help you get to know each other. Spend time having fun together—going on a picnic or cooking dinner together.

Worship and prayer. Your study will be enhanced by spending time praising God together in prayer or song. Pray for each other's needs—and keep track of how God is answering prayer in your group. Ask God to help you to apply what you are learning in your study.

Outreach. Reaching out to others can be a practical way of applying what you are learning, and it will keep your group from becoming self-focused. Host a series of evangelistic discussions for your friends or neighbors. Clean up the yard of an elderly friend. Serve at a soup kitchen together, or spend a day working in the community.

Many more suggestions and helps in each of these areas are found in the *Small Group Starter Kit*. You will also find information on building a small group. Reading through the starter kit will be worth your time.

Study 1. The God Who Shepherds Us. Psalm 23

Purpose: To experience God as our loving Shepherd.

General note. In the notes for each study you will find specific ideas for closing a group experience in prayer. Because of the personal nature of the psalm, you may want to have a time of silence for individual reflection and journaling before you pray together.

Question 1. David sees how his own sheep do not have to worry about anything because he is providing everything they need and planning ahead to meet their needs in the future. God who is powerful and loving is the one caring for us in this very personal way. We can rest in the truth that all that we need will be provided.

Question 2. This psalm describes several basic needs that God, our good Shepherd, provides for us. God provides food, water, rest, safety, guidance, his presence and comfort. God also provides protection, blessing and the gift of life with God here in this life and forever.

Question 3. Encourage participants to be honest as they reflect on this thought that God will provide everything we need. We can have a distorted idea about our needs. We may feel that we need to have certain physical features, or earn a certain income, or gain a certain level of success. We may think we need to "please" God by doing or achieving some level of faith or performance. This psalm takes us back to basic truths about who we are and what we really need and long for. With this renewed perspective, it can be deeply reassuring to reflect on the powerful statement this psalm makes. The Lord is our Shepherd. All our needs will be met. We can allow our hearts and minds and souls to be at rest.

Question 4. Allow time for group members to offer stories of the ways they see God's care in their lives in the past or in the present. You might respond to each one by simply thanking them for their story.

Question 5. Having our needs met in any of these ways can be a very moving and intimate experience. Sometimes it can be vulnerable to share these experiences. Treat this as a sacred trust as participants share their experiences of God's care.

Question 7. Again, encourage honesty. Many of us think of God as someone who expects too much of us. Perhaps we have heard that God has already given to us, and now it is our turn to give to God. Or perhaps we have distorted images of God and think of God as cruel or uncaring or withholding.

Question 8. We do not like to look at or admit our helplessness, our need, our vulnerabilities or our powerlessness. Yet, this is the starting place of Christian spirituality. It is the basis of true spiritual humility and wisdom. We are mortal creatures in need of our Maker's help and guidance. We are sheep. We need a loving Shepherd to provide for us.

Question 12. Allow a few minutes for people to reflect quietly. You might have people listen quietly as you reread the psalm and then allow them to take in whatever strikes them. Or they may want to picture God, their good Shepherd, offering them care. Invite participants to share whatever they want to share of their reflections.

Prayer. You may want to close the time together by inviting participants to write out their prayers, and then pray through them together.

Study 2. The God Who Invites Us to Rest. Matthew 11:25-30.

Purpose: To experience God, inviting us to rest.

Question 1. Invite participants to share personally about their reflections. Some may not be able to imagine such rest or any kind of rest.

Some may feel anxious when they think about rest. Some may feel peaceful or quieted.

Question 2. Spiritual pride leads us to depend on our own striving rather than on God's care and wisdom. Spiritual humility allows us to be aware of our limits and our needs, including our need to rest. In his prayer, Jesus acknowledges that our spiritual life is a gift from God. It cannot be earned or won in a competition. Our faith is something we receive from God. To be humble is to be receptive, open, childlike.

Question 3. Jesus' invitation to us in Matthew 11 is to come to him and to rest with him. Jesus goes on to invite us to take his yoke and discover it is light. And he invites us to learn of him (experience him) for he is gentle and humble.

Question 4. Jesus promises rest for our souls.

Question 5. Again, encourage participants to share honestly. Some may believe that Jesus wants and expects them to work harder, to strive, to do more and more. This invitation to true rest may be a surprise that is welcomed or that may be confusing.

Question 6. Jesus says he is gentle and humble of heart. These are powerful and surprising descriptions of the One who came to show us the face of God. Encourage participants to flesh out these two descriptions. What does it mean to be gentle? What does it mean to be humble?

Question 8. Rest for our souls is the deepest kind of rest possible. It is the assurance that we are known, that we are loved, that we are valued, that we are never alone because God—who is humble and gentle and who invites us to rest—is always with us.

Question 13. Give participants time to reflect and write. Invite those who want to share their experience in this time of reflection to do so.

Prayer. You might have participants write or pray quietly for a few minutes and then invite any who want to lead in prayer to do so.

Study 3. The God Who Guides Us. Psalm 25.

Purpose: To experience God as a good Shepherd, offering to guide us.

Question 1. The psalmist is experiencing fear of shame. Later (vv. 16-17) he says that he is lonely, afflicted, troubled and in anguish. He

also seems to be afraid for his life. There is an urgency and despera-
tion in his plea for help.

Question 3. The psalmist describes his relationship with God as one
of trust. He speaks of God's love for him and of God's goodness on
which he relies. He turns to God for forgiveness. He says his eyes are
always on the Lord. He counts on God's graciousness and responsive-
ness to him.

Question 4. Encourage participants to be honest and open by being
honest yourself about whatever struggles you may have with trusting
God and turning to God in these ways.

Question 5. The psalmist says that God is his Savior. He describes
God's great mercy and love. He says God is good. He describes God as
very active in our lives, instructing us, guiding us and teaching us. He
says that God is loving and faithful. He says that God confides in us,
that God makes God's covenant (God's heart, God's plans, God's grace,
God's desire for relationship) known to us. And he describes God as
One who releases us from snares, who rescues us and protects us.

Question 6. The psalmist asks God: do not let me be put to shame; show
me your ways; teach me your paths; guide me in your truth; remember
your great mercy and love; remember not the sins of my youth; remember me according to your great love; forgive my iniquity; turn to me and
be gracious to me; free me from my anguish; look upon my affliction and
my distress; take away my sins; see how my enemies have increased and
how they hate me; guard my life and rescue me; let integrity and upright-
ness protect me; redeem Israel from all their troubles.

Question 9. God's guidance is always guidance to love. Loving ways
are the right paths (or paths of righteousness) that God desires to lead
us on. Our sin is a result of our choosing to walk paths that are less
than loving. We need God to heal and forgive our waywardness and to
teach us and guide us in God's way of love.

Prayer. Invite the group to pray for themselves and for each other
regarding specific guidance they need from God.

Study 4. The God Who Is with Us. Psalm 34.

Purpose: To experience God's presence with us.

Question 1. The purpose of this question is to help participants gain an overview of the text. The themes have to do with God's care and deliverance in times of trouble, and with the wisdom of seeking God's help and living according to God's guidance. The central theme is stated in verse 2: "My soul will boast in the Lord, let the afflicted hear and rejoice."

Question 2. David says that God answered him (v. 4), delivered him from all his fears (v. 4), made his face radiant (v. 5), saved him out of all his troubles (v. 6), sent his angel to be with him and deliver him (v. 7), is close to the brokenhearted (v. 18), saves those who are crushed in spirit (v. 18), protects his bones (v. 20) and redeems his servants (v. 22).

Question 3. David's response to God's help and deliverance is passionate gratitude and praise.

Question 5. David offers us wisdom for living. He instructs us to "taste and see that the LORD is good." He tells us that we will be blessed and rescued if we take refuge in God. David goes on to describe specifics of righteous living: keep your tongue from evil and your lips from lies, turn from evil and do good, and seek peace and pursue it.

Question 7. Invite participants to be honest about their experiences. Have they felt God's presence in some way in times of trouble or not? Have they seen God deliver them in some way or not? Do they feel disappointed by God or helped by God?

Prayer. Invite the group to share their gratitude and their troubles with each other and with God.

Study 5. The God Who Comforts Us. Isaiah 40:9-11, 25-31.

Purpose: To experience the comfort of God.

Question 1. The good tidings are that God is powerful, God is loving, and God actively intervenes to help and provide. The specific good news that Isaiah was declaring was that God who is loving and powerful will bring his people out of exile and restore them to their homeland.

Question 2. God is the sovereign Lord who comes with power. And God is a tender shepherd who carries us close to his heart. God is the One who is incomparable in power and strength. And God is One who understands, who cares about our needs, who gives strength to the weak.

Question 3. Encourage participants to reflect on this text and on its personal impact on them as they read and re-read it.

Questions 8-9. Allow time for participants to reflect quietly. Invite them to share their reflections.

Question 10. Spend some time reflecting on the images of being weary and of stumbling and falling. And then spend time contrasting these images with the images of being strengthened by hope in the Lord—to soar and run and walk.

Prayer. You might want to preface your prayer time with a time of silent reflection as described under "Now or Later." Invite participants to talk to each other and to God about their specific needs for God's comfort at this time in their lives, and to thank God for the ways they are experiencing God's comfort.

Study 6. The God Who Feeds Us. Isaiah 55.

Purpose: To experience God as the One who nurtures and feeds us.

Question 1. Many people do not think of God in this way, as a loving, nurturing God. Encourage participants to reflect honestly about what this awareness of God might mean to them on a daily basis.

Question 2. Our enemies might be actual people who judge us or shame us or attack us spiritually in some way. A "spiritual enemy" might be any life situation that causes our heart to fear. Spiritual enemies might also be our despair or self-rejection that drive us away from God's nurture and care. And spiritual enemies might be obsessions or addictions that promise to satisfy us but which only lead to emptiness and ruin. Encourage participants to explore who the possible spiritual enemies might be in their lives.

Question 4. Take a few minutes to picture this experience and to talk about what it would feel like.

Question 5. This text urges us to come to God and find the nourishment we are hungry for. God is the One who offers us water, milk and wine free of charge. God is the One who offers our souls the richest of fare. God is a God of faithful love, who endows us with splendor, who has mercy on us and freely pardons us. God's ways are higher than our ways; God's thoughts are higher than our thoughts. God's Word is powerful and true and accomplishes the purpose of God. God is the One who promises us joy.

Question 6. This text has an urgency to it. God is inviting us, imploring us, to make choices that are good for us, that will satisfy our deepest desires. This text invites and instructs us to come to God. We are thirsty and have no money. We are invited to come to God for water, milk and wine. We are instructed to listen to God and to eat what is good. We are instructed to seek the Lord while he may be found and to call on him while he is near.

Question 8. The "good" that God wants to feed us is found in the text. God offers us faithful love (v. 3), mercy and pardon (v. 7), joy and peace (v. 12).

Question 10. When our deepest desire for God's nurturing love is being met, we know that we are loved, valued and safe in God's care. Our hearts fill with gratitude and joy. Encourage participants to reflect on times when they have experienced this.

Prayer. Spend some time praying together as a group for gifts of hunger for God and a deeper capacity to receive from God.

Study 7. The God Who Heals Us. Isaiah 61:1-3.

Purpose: To experience God as the God who heals.

Question 1. The purpose of this question is to help participants gain an overview of the text. Encourage a variety of possible titles. One possible title might be "A Portrait of God's Anointed." Another might be "A Picture of God's Active, Healing Love."

Question 2. This text describes God's anointed One preaching good news to the poor, binding up the brokenhearted, proclaiming freedom to captives, releasing prisoners from darkness and comforting all who mourn.

Question 3. Encourage participants to reflect on the life, ministry and teachings of Jesus, as well as his death and resurrection. Name specific ways in which he demonstrated God's active healing love for humankind.

Question 6. Encourage participants to reflect honestly on the ways their sense of God may match and may not match the remarkable portrayal of God in this text.

Question 7. The "before" picture is a picture of someone in active mourning. The person is grieving, has ashes on their head and feels despair. The "after" picture is the picture of someone who has been comforted. They now are wearing a crown of beauty on their head, anointed with oil of gladness and dressed in a garment of praise. **Questions 8-9.** These are both pictures of joy. When we allow ourselves to grieve and to take in God's comfort, the result is healing and joy. Encourage participants to share their experiences of joy when healing has come. **Prayer.** You may want to use the first exercise in the "Now or Later" section to close your time. Allow time for personal reflection and writing, followed by discussion and prayer.

Study 8. The God Who Blesses Us. Psalm 40.
Purpose: To experience God as the God who blesses us.
Question 2. God turned to David, heard his cry, lifted him out of the pit, set his feet on a rock, gave him a firm place to stand and put a new song in his heart.
Question 6. These verses are talking about David's realization that God is not looking for religious behaviors. God is not concerned with performance. God invites and longs for true relationship with us.
Questions 9-10. Allow a time of quiet work and then in question 10 invite participants to share their gratitude lists with the group.
Prayer. You might want to use the gratitude lists to directly thank God for his goodness and love.

Study 9. The God Who Is Our True Home. Psalm 16.
Purpose: To experience God as our true home.
Question 1. The psalmist says that God is his safe refuge (v. 1), the one good thing in life (v. 2), his provider (v. 5), his counselor (v. 7), his teacher and guide in life (vv. 8, 11), and always with him (v. 8).
Question 2. Psalm 16 is another intimate portrait of David's relationship with God. God is not some abstract idea to David. God is the source of David's joy. God speaks to David and counsels him. God is David's refuge. God is always with David, providing and guiding and caring for him.

Question 4. David seems to be saying that his fellow believers are a delight to him. God is his refuge and home, and other believers are an important part of this experience of "home."

Question 6. The sense of God as David's true home here in this life is very strong in the psalm. God is our refuge. God is the one good thing in life. God is with us by night, counseling us, and by day God is at our right hand. God makes known to us the path of life and fills us with joy in his presence. It is a picture of heaven on earth.

Question 10. David states that God will not abandon him to the grave (v. 10). And David looks forward to eternal pleasures at God's right hand (v. 11).

Question 11. The psalmist responds to God with joy and gratitude, with eagerness to hear God's counsel, with the ability to rest secure.

Question 12. You might want to simply read Psalm 23 out loud and then give the group a few minutes to meditate on God, and on the image of dwelling with God forever.

Prayer. You might want to close this study with a time of expressing thanksgiving for God who is our good Shepherd.

Juanita Ryan is a clinical nurse specialist with an MSN in psychiatric mental health nursing, which she has taught at Bethel University, Rio Hondo Community College and Biola University. She is currently a therapist in private practice at Brea Family Counseling Center in Brea, California. Juanita is also the author of the LifeBuilder Bible Studies Waiting for God, Busyness *and* Praying the Psalms. *Together with her husband, Dale, she authored* Distorted Images of Self, *also published in this series.*